Ding-Dong
Pizza!

by Frances Ann Ladd

Illustrated by Duendes del Sur

D0888271

SCHOLASTIC INC.

New York   Toronto   London   Auckland   Sydney
Mexico City   New Delhi   Hong Kong   Buenos Aires

Scooby and Shaggy had a job bringing pizzas to people.

"Scooby, we have to
bring a pizza
to that creepy house,"
Shaggy said.
Shaggy did not want
to go and ring the bell.
"You ring it," he said.

Scooby's heart sank. He clung to Shaggy. "Do you think we can just honk the horn?" Shaggy said.

They walked up to
the door.
Shaggy sang a little song:
"Ring, ring,
ring the bell.
Ding, dong,
ding the bell."

Shaggy stuck out
his finger.
He stopped.
"Scoob, I do not think
I can bring myself
to ring that bell!"
They slunk back
to the van.

"Jeepers!" said Shaggy.
"We have been
sitting here
a long time.
I am hungry!
I can't stand
being hungry
any longer."

Scooby opened
the pizza box.
He winked at Shaggy.
"Good thinking, Scoob.
We are working hard.
We should eat the pizza!"
"Right!" said Scooby.

They ate the whole thing.